The Garments of

PRAISE

Jose Matias Rojas

ISBN - 9798865349600

CreateSpace Independent Publishing Platform

MORE International Ministries

Evangelist Matias Rojas

1 Main St. Terryville, CT 06786

https://www.miministries.org

Scriptures are taken from the King James Version.

Contents

Dedicated to my Lord and Savior Jesus Christ
to Whom be glory, honor, and praise
forever and ever. Amen!

Introduction

When I first came to Jesus, I understood that there were many things I had to let go of. I was entangled with the things of the world: bad friends, evil speaking, and sinful actions. Leaving those things was not a problem for me compared to leaving the love I had for music.

I asked the Lord to reveal to me why I had such a hard time letting go of my music. I was attracted to so many different kinds of music! According to my mother, when I was young, I used to dance a lot in school, starting when I was six years old. I'm Hispanic, so I grew up listening to Salsa, Merengue, and Bachata. The music that most influenced me throughout my whole life was hip-hop which I was introduced to when I came to the United States in 1998.

I noticed that after my conversion, one of the

things that many of my friends asked about was the fact that I no longer listened to rap music. They couldn't imagine that I could give up something that I loved so much. I have to say that this is the number one reason why so many teenagers have not come to Christ yet. The Prince of the Air, through his musical ability, has been able to capture their inherent desire to praise and then turn it in the wrong direction. So the Lord started ministering to me that the reason why so many young people have a hard time leaving their worldly music behind them is that they were created to praise!

In sixteen short and easy-to-read chapters let me share with you what our Lord Jesus has revealed to me about our Garments of Praise!

Matias Rojas

1
Created To Praise

We are clothed with what the Prophet Isaiah calls the garments of praise. In Isaiah 43:21 the Lord speaks through the Prophet saying,

This people have I formed for myself; they shall shew forth my praise.

God is letting us know that we were created to praise somebody. It is engrained in us to sing. I can't help but lift my voice to somebody every day. That's why the Psalmist says in Psalm 22:3,

But thou art holy, O thou that inhabitest the praises of Israel.

These were the words of David (by the Holy Spirit), letting us know that God's perfect plan for us is for Him to constantly remain with us. The word inhabit comes from the Hebrew word "yashab" which means to sit down, dwell, and remain. In the very beginning Adam and Eve experienced perfect communion with the Father before the fall. The reason why the Bible says that they saw themselves naked in Genesis, Chapter Three was that they previously were clothed with the garments of praise.

And the eyes of them both were opened, and they knew that they were naked. (3:7)

Those garments were replaced by another set of garments, which were natural ones. When they were clothed with the garments of praise, God inhabited the praises of His people. As long as they praised God, God dwelt inside of them and with them. They dwelt in God's promise and God's presence.

Notice what happened next. These garments were replaced with a spirit of heaviness. They were kicked out of the Garden because of their sinful choices. And when they chose sin, they stopped praising Him. When we stop praising God, we no longer can stay in His presence. As soon as they lost their garments, the Lord stopped inhabiting with them. And the angels took their place according to Revelation 4:8: **"And they rest not day and night, saying, 'Holy, holy, holy, Lord God Almighty, which was, and is, and is to come.'"**

The prophet Isaiah describes this incident in Isaiah 61:3, describing when Jesus comes back to revert or bring back the people of God to their original state which our forefathers lost. Listen to what he says:

To appoint unto them that mourn in Zion, to

give unto them beauty for ashes, the oil of joy for mourning, the garments of praise for the spirit of heaviness; that they might be called trees of righteousness, the planting of the Lord, that He might be glorified.

2

The Exchange

When our forefather Adam sinned, we all lost the garments of praise which were replaced by the spirit of heaviness. The word heaviness from the Hebrew word "keheh" which means obscure darkness. Understandably, so many musicians in the world can't help but rap about dark things. They were created to praise, but another spirit is now driving them to lift praises to the Prince of the Air.

Adam and Eve were reclothed with fig leaves in Genesis 3:7;

And they sewed fig leaves together and made themselves aprons.

They reclothed themselves with new garments,

but note that these were leaves that came from trees where the serpent dwelt. The world cannot help but praise the enemy because they have been reclothed with what he dwells in: darkness. They were reclothed with leaves which is the dwelling place of the enemy. The enemy, which is represented by the snake, hides in the leaves and in the darkness.

3

Don't Allow Him to Grab Your Praise

There is a divine power that's driving us to praise. When the enemy grabs your praise, he can lock you up in jail and accuse you before God because God commanded in Psalm 150:6:

Let everything that hath breath praise the Lord. Praise ye the Lord.

This was not an option, but rather, a commandment. The enemy wants to grab our praise so God will not dwell with us. In doing so, he puts us in a spiritual prison. Do you remember the story about Joseph and how Potiphar's wife wanted to lay with him and he refused? Genesis 39:12-16:

She caught him by his garment, saying, "Lie with me:" and he left his garment in her hand, and fled, and got him out. And it came to pass, when she saw that he had left his garment in her hand, and was fled forth, that she called unto the men of her house, and spake unto them, saying, "See, he hath brought in an Hebrew unto us to mock us; he came in unto me to lie with me, and I cried with a loud voice: And it came to pass, when he heard that I lifted up my voice and cried, that he left his garment with me, and fled, and got him out." And she laid up his garment by her, until his lord came home.

Understand that this is a perfect illustration of what happens when the enemy grabs your garments of praise. He goes up before the presence of God and accuses the brethren before God in order to have them thrown into jail. The enemy wants to be like The Most High. His greatest desire, just like God, is to receive honor and praise. The number one thing that God receives is glory and praise! He is The Most High and everything that has breath should praise the Lord.

When the enemy can keep your mouth shut so you do not praise God in any circumstance (whether at home, in personal trial, or financial difficulties) he is mocking God. He is telling God, "The person you created in Your image and likeness, instead of praising You amid the circumstance, is keeping quiet and thus praising me and the circumstance;" and thereby ridiculing God. Doing this fulfills the words he said in Isaiah 14:12-14:

How art thou fallen from heaven, O Lucifer, son of the morning! how art thou cut down to the ground, which didst weaken the nations!

For thou hast said in thine heart, "I will ascend into heaven, I will exalt my throne above the stars of God: I will sit also upon the mount of the congregation, in the sides of the north: I will ascend above the heights of the clouds; I will be like the most High."

Understand that Lucifer wants God to know that he is greater than Him because the people God created, who look exactly like Him, are praising Lucifer rather than God. He wishes to mock God through the praise of God's people being towards him.

4

Praise Turned His Back

Do you remember what happened in heaven when Lucifer the arch-praiser betrayed God?

Thou art the anointed cherub that covereth; and I have set thee so: thou wast upon the holy mountain of God; thou hast walked up and down in the midst of the stones of fire. Thou wast perfect in thy ways from the day that thou wast created, till iniquity was found in thee. (Ezekiel 28:14-15)

The word covereth here means to shield or protect. It demonstrated that Lucifer was very close to God in glory, yet he was the one that led the rebellion of the angels against God in heaven. It is not a coincidence that the chief musician in heaven betrayed God and that the name of the one that betrayed Jesus was Judas. The name Judas means "praise" because it originates from the Hebrew word "whudah" which means Judah. The word Judah means to celebrate. God was betrayed, both in glory as well as in His earthly ministry, by that which celebrated Him. Accordingly, Jesus had to be betrayed by a kiss because it was a common way of greeting one another in love in those times. So Judas, showing that he was celebrating Him with love, was actually the enemy ridiculing God, showing everyone that through intimacy he betrayed Him.

So you must understand that the enemy has always attempted to hit God where it hurts Him the most: in praise. For this reason, Lucifer betrayed Him in glory because he understood the power that is revealed when the angels and the people of God praise Him. Notice that in heaven nothing else is required but to praise God. It talks about how a group in heaven sang a new song about how everything done in glory by the angels, elders, and people of God is constant praise.

Revelation 14:2-3: **And I heard a voice from heaven, as the voice of many waters, and as the voice of a great thunder: and I heard the voice of harpers harping with their harps: And they sung as it were a new song before the throne, and before the four beasts, and the elders: and no man could learn that song but the hundred and forty and four thousand, which were redeemed from the earth.**

This teaches us that the group singing the new song was privileged to praise God in a new, intimate way while the others who were unaware of the song still praised God.

5
Judah!

Everybody in glory praises the King of Kings and Lord of Lords. Nothing else is required. It is a constant celebration that stems from the word Judah, which means celebrated. I want to give you some background on this man named Judah. Genesis 29:35 says this child was the fourth child that was born to Jacob and Leah. Understand that he came after Levi.

She conceived again and bore a son, and said, "Now this time my husband will become attached to me, because I have borne him three sons." Therefore his name was called Levi. And she conceived again and bore a son, and said, "Now I will praise the Lord." Therefore she called his name Judah. Then

she stopped bearing. (NKJV)

The Lord wanted to show us in these two verses that once you are joined to your husband, the one that comes after is praise. Levi had to come before Judah. The husband represents God, and Leah represents the church. Levi was the forefather of Aaron. Aaron was the one that was the first High Priest to go into the Holy of Holies to be a mediator in joining God and His people Israel. Once the offering was accepted and he came out alive, all the people could do was to praise. This is why Judah was Leah's last son.

Once you have offered up your prayer to God and believe He has accepted it, you must praise Him as if it were already done. The Scriptures say that Judah was their last son and she was left barren. This demonstrates that praising Him is the last thing you have to do.

So Judah is a key person in the Old Testament. I want to remind you that it was Judah who spoke to Jacob to allow Benjamin, his youngest son, to come through the desert into Egypt to see Joseph, the Prince of Egypt.

And Judah said unto Israel his father, "Send the lad with me, and we will arise and go; that we may live, and not die, both we, and thou, and also our little ones. I will be surety for him; of my hand shalt thou require him: if I bring him not unto thee, and set him before thee, then let me bear the blame for ever." (Genesis 43:8-9)

While Jacob did not allow any other son to take Benjamin, he did allow Judah to take the lad. It was praise that spoke up, and Jacob, demonstrating his trust in Judah (praise), allowed him to take the most precious thing he had left through the desert and into Egypt. This privilege was not even allowed to Rueben, the firstborn, or to Levi, the thirdborn.

6

A Heart of Praise

Israel (Jacob) represents God and the desert and Egypt represents the low and dry times in your life. Only praise can take you through this. Recall what David said in the famous Psalm 23:4:

Yea, though I walk through the valley of the shadow of death, I will fear no evil: for Thou art with me; Thy rod and Thy staff they comfort me.

David understood that as he went through valleys, as long as he kept praising God, the Lord had to come down and inhabit his praises. That is why David declared in Psalm 34:1:

I will bless the Lord at all times: His praise shall continually be in my mouth.

David understood something about praise that many of us do not understand. For this reason God says in 1 Samuel 16:1:

The Lord said unto Samuel, "How long wilt thou mourn for Saul, seeing I have rejected him from reigning over Israel? fill thine horn with oil, and go, I will send thee to Jesse the Bethlehemite: for I have provided me a king among his sons."

David was a man considered by God to have a heart after God's own heart. Even though everybody looked at David as just a kid, God saw a king because David was a constant praiser. Praise Him!

7

The Enemy Does Not Want to Hear Your Music

We have read what David said in the Psalms.

I will bless the Lord at all times; His praise shall continually be in my mouth. (Psalm 34:1)

It is not a coincidence that David destroyed a giant, never lost a war, and overcame many kingdoms. While Saul killed thousands, David killed ten thousand. This is what the enemy fears and what God desires for you to find out how David was so powerful. David knew so much about the power of always wearing the garments of praise. The enemy is scared of you learning how to operate this mighty tool. Yes, it was praise to God that helped David destroy the lion and the bear. It was praise that the enemy could not withstand every time David was in a war. Listen to what happened in 1 Samuel:

> Saul's servants said unto him, "Behold now, an evil spirit from God troubleth thee. Let our lord now command thy servants, which are before thee, to seek out a man, who is a cunning player on an harp: and it shall come to pass, when the evil spirit from God is upon thee, that he shall play with his hand, and thou shalt be well." And Saul said unto his servants, "Provide me now a man that can play well, and bring him to me." (16:15-17) Then verse 23 says:

> And it came to pass, when the evil spirit from God was upon Saul, that David took an harp, and played with his hand: so Saul was refreshed, and was well, and the evil spirit departed from him.

As you can see in the Scripture, the enemy doesn't want you to find out that Saul represents those who have been enslaved by the enemy. David represents the church which has the power in its praise to refresh those who have been enslaved by the enemy. Saul represents Egypt (the world), the evil spirit represents Lucifer (who is ultimately controlled by God). Lucifer is the one who hovers over the nations to torment. Yet, with one sold-out, God-filled praiser, he must leave and depart from those he has bound. That is why he wants you to wear the garments of praise because he knows that if you release the praise of God from within you, God will descend and begin releasing those who are bound.

8

The Key Is Praise

Let's look at Paul and Silas in prison in the book of Acts 16:23-26:

And when they had laid many stripes upon them, they cast them into prison, charging the jailor to keep them safely: who, having received such a charge, thrust them into the inner prison, and made their feet fast in the stocks. And at midnight Paul and Silas prayed, and sang praises unto God: and the prisoners heard them. And suddenly there was a great earthquake, so that the foundations of the prison were shaken: and immediately all the doors were opened, and every one's bands were loosed.

The prison is the place where all those who have not found Christ are bound by the enemy. The enemy desires to put all those who preach the Gospel in the inner prison where Paul and Silas were bound by their feet. Midnight represents the start of a new day, even though it is the darkest point of the night.

The first thing that Paul and Silas prayed to God for was their deliverance, but nothing happened. When they started praising Him and lifting Him up, He had to come to where they were and inhabit their praises. So the words of the Psalmist have to be fulfilled:

In Thy presence is fulness of joy, (Psalm 16:11) and in the fulness of joy there is freedom!

When God came into the prison, He had to free up those who were praising Him and also free up those who were listening about Him. Prayers detonate explosions in the spirit. There was such a great earthquake that the foundations of the prison were shaken. The prison was where the captives of the enemy were bound. It was shaken because the Prince of the Air cannot withstand the praises of the church. At the sound of true praise going up, immediately all doors in the spirit of those held captive are opened and every single one of their bands are loosed.

9

The Power of Agreement

It is the job of the church to bring God and those who are in the world together. In the same way, Jesus' job is to be our Mediator. Understand that Jesus came through the lineage of Judah. It was praise that brought Him into the world. It has not changed. It is still praise that is going to bring Him down into the church to set the captives free. The Scriptures calls Him the Lion of Judah, and He said in John 14:12:

Verily, verily, I say unto you, He that believeth on me, the works that I do shall he do also; and greater works than these shall he do; because I go unto my Father.

His job was to unite humanity with divinity. The word lion means king of the jungle. We know Judah means praise, symbolizing that high praise is going to join together humanity and divinity. The same job has now been left to the church. That is why the early church was so successful.

And they, continuing daily with one accord in the temple, and breaking bread from house to house, did eat their meat with gladness and singleness of heart, praising God, and having favour with all the people. And the Lord added to the church daily such as should be saved. (Acts 2:46-47)

Many of us do part of what the early church did. We come in one accord and break bread together, but we have forgotten to praise God. This was the last thing that they did in every single one of their meetings, causing them to have favor with all men and the Lord adding those that needed to be saved.

God has healed many of us who were crippled in various ways, just like the man who was lame in the third chapter of Acts. This man went daily to the temple's gate which is called Beautiful, in order to ask for alms. The Bible registers in the 8th verse:

And he leaping up stood, and walked, and entered with them into the temple, walking, and leaping, and praising God.

We have gotten up in the spirit but have forgotten to go back into the temple, like this man, to praise God. We are like the ten lepers that were healed and then went about their way in the Gospel of Luke. Only one returned to give thanks and worship the Lord. Jesus asked, "Were there not ten that were made healed? Where are the nine? You have returned; now you are made whole."

Prayer starts to give you victory, but it was at their request that they were healed. It was praise that completed the job which was demonstrated by the one grateful leper who returned to give thanks.

10

Shout!

It appeared to be an impossible task. How were
Joshua and his army going to conquer a walled
city like Jericho? Joshua, Chapter 6:3-9 says,

**"Ye shall compass the city, all ye men of war,
and go round about the city once. Thus shalt
thou do six days. And seven priests shall bear
before the ark seven trumpets of rams' horns:
and the seventh day ye shall compass the city
seven times, and the priests shall blow with
the trumpets. And it shall come to pass, that
when they make a long blast with the ram's
horn, and when ye hear the sound of the
trumpet, all the people shall shout with a
great shout; and the wall of the city shall fall**

down flat, and the people shall ascend up every man straight before him." And Joshua the son of Nun called the priests, and said unto them, "Take up the ark of the covenant, and let seven priests bear seven trumpets of rams' horns before the ark of the Lord." And he said unto the people, "Pass on, and compass the city, and let him that is armed pass on before the ark of the Lord." And it came to pass, when Joshua had spoken unto the people, that the seven priests bearing the seven trumpets of rams' horns passed on before the Lord, and blew with the trumpets: and the ark of the covenant of the Lord followed them. And the armed men went before the priests that blew with the trumpets, and the rereward came after the ark, the priests going on, and blowing with the trumpets.

So they followed those divine instructions:

Verse 15-17: **And it came to pass on the seventh day, that they rose early about the dawning of the day, and compassed the city after the same manner seven times: only on that day they compassed the city seven times. And it came to pass at the seventh time, when the priests blew with the trumpets, Joshua said unto the people, "Shout; for the Lord hath given you the city. And the city shall be accursed, even it, and all that are therein, to the Lord: only Rahab the harlot shall live, she and all that are with her in the house, because she hid the messengers that we sent."**

God commanded the Prophet Joshua to set seven priests with the seven trumpets before the ark of the covenant. The number seven means perfection and for this reason, there had to be seven priests. God wanted the church to know that if He got the right amount of praisers, He would come behind them.

Notice that there were armed men before the seven priests. These armed men went before them in prayer while the priest constantly praised with the seven trumpets.

On the seventh day, they got up around dawn and compassed the city seven times. This illustration helps us understand that if you can hold fast to your blessing until the appointed time comes, you will receive what God has promised you.

The wall of Jericho was the most fortified barrier during this time period. Since the enemy knew their Promised Land lay beyond Jericho, he made it impossible for anyone to come in or go out. This is the state in which the world is right now. The enemy has built a wall around their hearts so nothing can get in or out. They are too bound to get out by themselves and the walls are too big for others to penetrate and go get them. Therefore God's Spirit, which only comes after the praisers, must be sent.

God has shown us the key to destroying that wall.

The armed men went ahead praying, and the priests came behind them praising. However, it was at the united shout of all the priests, armed men, and people that the presence of the Lord was forced to come down. There is a powerful deliverance that takes place in the spirit when you can get a group of praisers united to give God the glory.

Know this: the Promised Land is the soul of every human. The walls of Jericho are the demons wrapped around the souls to keep them separated from God. But at the sound of the people of God praising, He has to come and put the enemy under His feet! That is why the walls collapsed; God had descended in response to His people's praises, making all His enemies His footstool.

Some of you are familiar with Matthew 18:19 which says,

Again I say unto you, that if two of you shall agree on earth as touching any thing that they

shall ask, it shall be done for them of my Father which is in heaven.

Here is a profound revelation of the Scripture. The word agree comes from the Greek text and means "harmonist." The word harmonist is translated into the word harmony. The word harmony means a group that is in one accord with instruments and sounds. The word accord is a two-part word (ar) represents array and the word (cord) is for chorus representing that if God can find a chorus that will array themselves on the frontlines, they will have whatever they asked of the Lord. Praise the Lord!

11
Praise Speaks For Itself

God was saying when He can get a group that will establish praise within them, He will do wonders in their midst. That is what we see happening in 2 Chronicles 20:22. When the enemy came up against King Jehosphat, he and his people began to praise God in the midst of the danger. We see how God confused their enemies. This is a secret that God wants us to live our lives on earth by. The more we praise God, the more confused the enemy becomes.

And when they began to sing and to praise, the Lord set ambushments against the children of Ammon, Moab, and mount Seir, which were come against Judah; and they

THE GARMENTS OF PRAISE

were smitten.

Jehosphat had told the people earlier that morning,

Believe in the Lord your God, so shall ye be established; believe his prophets, so shall ye prosper.

The word established means, "unmovable; standing on solid ground." We are on solid ground what we gather in His Name to praise Him! Matthew 18:20 says,

For where two or three are gathered together in my name, there am I in the midst of them.

The Lord desires a people who will establish praise within them. The reason David never lost a battle was because no matter how many armed men went to battle with him, he never forgot to establish praise unto God so that God would be forced to be in his presence. That gave him the victory every time.

God just needs a few believers in this time to get together and start lifting Him up and every battle will be won. God doesn't need you to do much. He is Omni (all) potent (powerful). Listen to how important praising was to David according to 1 Chronicles 23:5:

Moreover four thousand were porters; and four thousand praised the Lord with the instruments which I made, said David, to praise therewith.

David understood clearly that prayer started the war, but it was praise that finished it. He went before with armed men into war, but it was the four thousand hidden praisers that gave them the victory. God had to inhabit the praises of his people. Praise causes God to remember you in time of need and war. God commanded Moses in Numbers 10:2:

Make thee two trumpets of silver; of a whole piece shalt thou make them: that thou mayest use them for the calling of the assembly, and for the journeying of the camps.

Understand that these two trumpets had to be of silver because it represents purified praise; meaning praise that is willing to withstand the fire. They had to be a whole piece representing a soul that has been made whole by the Lord. Recognize that God is trying to tell us when we put our whole trust in Him, we are going to have available the whole assembly. He is not talking about a natural assembly. This was written for our learning, to teach us what happens in the spirit every time we praise. The assembly of glory is made available for a true praiser.

It is for this reason the walls of Jericho had to come down. The angels in glory came to assist in that war. It is for this reason the foundations of the prison were shaken in Acts. Heaven came to assist them while they were in prison. Remember that the Lord said unto Joshua, "I am the captain of the Lord's Hosts." The word "host" means multitudes. So when you bring Jesus into the midst through your praise, you bring the whole host of heaven with Jesus.

Remember what happened when Jesus was born in Luke 2:10-13:

The angel said unto them, "Fear not: for, behold, I bring you good tidings of great joy, which shall be to all people. For unto you is born this day in the city of David a Saviour, which is Christ the Lord. And this shall be a sign unto you; ye shall find the babe wrapped

in swaddling clothes, lying in a manger." And suddenly there was with the angel a multitude of the heavenly host praising God.

This is a description of what happens every time you draw Jesus to earth. He does not come by Himself. There is always a multitude of the heavenly hosts accompanying Him. So every time you praise God, you are drawing in God and all of heaven with Him. Not only is praise doing this for you, but remember what the Lord said to Moses at the latter end of the verse in Numbers 10:2:

Make thee two trumpets of silver; of a whole piece shalt thou make them: that thou mayest use them for the calling of the assembly, and for the journeying of the camps.

This lets you know that moving through the

desert and into the Promised Land is going to be based on your praise. It is going to be based upon how fast you're willing to praise Him after you have come to a stop in your spiritual walk or into a dry place.

If Paul and Silas had started at 11pm and not midnight, they would have gotten out of jail earlier. It was based on their praise that God came to get them out. God wants you to know He is a just God and is going to give to every man according to their works.

Do you remember the story about blind Bartimaeus, when he heard that Jesus was passing by? He started crying out, **"Jesus, Thou son of David, have mercy on me."** (Mark 10:47) Though the people told him to hold his peace, he cried out even more. His praise stopped Jesus from doing what He was going to do and pay attention to him because your praise was given to you so that God could remember you.

God has blessings for everyone but bear in mind, He is a just God. Though He has a blessing for everyone, only those that acknowledge Him are going to receive it. Your praise was given to you so whenever you want or need God's attention, you can get it. Notice what He says in Numbers 10:9:

And if ye go to war in your land against the enemy that oppresseth you, then ye shall blow an alarm with the trumpets; and ye shall be remembered before the Lord your God, and ye shall be saved from your enemies.

Blind Bartimaeus, sounded the alarm in the spirit. He knew something that no other lame person knew: that when you sound the alarm in praise, God is forced to remember you. This represents that God is always passing by our lives, but it is only our praise that is going to stop Him. Now, I dare you to stop God!

12

Praise Keeps You Alive

B lind Bartimaeus was at war with blindness. He could not see the King of Glory. This represents spiritual death. But upon praising God, he forced God to bring him back to life. Notice what Jesus asked him:

"What wilt thou that I should do unto thee?" The blind man said unto him, "Lord, that I might receive my sight." And Jesus said unto him, "Go thy way; thy faith hath made thee whole." And immediately he received his sight, and followed Jesus in the way. (Mark 10:52-53)

His praise had brought him back to life by getting

God's attention upon him. Praise will not only bring you back to life, it will keep you alive as well. Have you read the story about King Hezekiah?

In those days was Hezekiah sick unto death. And Isaiah the prophet the son of Amoz came unto him, and said unto him, "Thus saith the Lord, Set thine house in order: for thou shalt die, and not live." Then Hezekiah turned his face toward the wall, and prayed unto the Lord, and said, "Remember now, O Lord, I beseech thee, how I have walked before thee in truth and with a perfect heart, and have done that which is good in thy sight." And Hezekiah wept sore. Then came the word of the Lord to Isaiah, saying, "Go, and say to Hezekiah, Thus saith the Lord, the God of David thy father, I have heard thy prayer, I have seen thy tears: behold, I will add unto thy days fifteen years." (Isaiah 38:1-6)

The prophet had come with a word from God, declaring that God had spoken, "You shall die." Notice it was not the enemy, neither was it a man. I asked the Lord to show me why He changed His mind within a few minutes about the declaration He had just made as the prophet Isaiah declared King Hezekiah's death. What was it that made God change His mind in that prayer? Isaiah 38 verse 9 says,

The writing of Hezekiah king of Judah, when he had been sick, and was recovered of his sickness.

God revealed that it was King Hezekiah's prayer that caused God to change His mind. Listen closely to how Hezekiah finished his life-altering prayer:

For the grave cannot praise thee, death can not celebrate thee: they that go down into the pit cannot hope for thy truth. The living, the living, he shall praise thee, as I do this day: the father to the children shall make known thy truth.

These are the final words of King Hezekiah's prayer. Now do you understand why God had to add 15 years onto his life? God thought within Himself, "If I take this man's life, he can't praise Me nor celebrate Me." The Lord told Isaiah, "Turn back. I'm going to give him another 15 years to praise Me. It was the fact that the living are the only ones that can praise God and Hezekiah was a constant praiser. God did not have a choice but to add unto him another 15 years. This is the word of the living God upon you: "Sound the trumpet, and I have to remember you."

Those that have a need, a sickness, a pain in your

head or your body, or if someone in your family is still not saved, take some time right now to just praise God. The Lord is going to heal you right now. Make sure to let your praise be bigger than your need, so that God may remember you and keep you alive!

13

The Garments of Praise

God's Word had been established from the beginning, making praise the number one thing that keeps us alive. In Exodus 28:33 notice the commandment that God gave Moses to give unto Aaron and his sons:

> **And beneath upon the hem of it thou shalt make pomegranates of blue, and of purple, and of scarlet, round about the hem thereof; and bells of gold between them round about: A golden bell and a pomegranate, a golden bell and a pomegranate, upon the hem of the robe round about. And it shall be upon Aaron to minister: and his sound shall be heard when he goeth in unto the holy place before**

the Lord, and when he cometh out, that he die not.

Pay close attention to the latter end of this verse.

And his sound shall be heard when he goeth in unto the holy place before the Lord, and when he cometh out, that he die not.

God is so jealous about His praise that when He saw that man was weak in his flesh, he integrated a sound into Aaron's garments. Every time Aaron opened his voice before God, God could hear the bells and not kill him. Praise is so important that the Psalmist said, **"Enter into his gates with thanksgiving, and into his courts with praise."** (Psalm 100:4) A lot of us stop there. The High Priest dared not enter into the most holy place without praising Him, because he could die.

As we consider the bottom of his garment, we notice there were bells with pomegranates. Pomegranates are fruit and the bells are for sound or praise. You might be wondering why the fruits and bells had to be at the end of his garments. The apostle Paul in Hebrews 13:15 says,

By him therefore let us offer the sacrifice of praise to God continually, that is, the fruit of our lips giving thanks to His name.

Notice the combination between Exodus and Hebrews. God placed fruits and bells to go together at the bottom of the hem of Aaron's garments. This was only a representation of the fruit of our lips giving thanks to His name continuously. God knew Aaron would forget to give Him the fruit of his lips one day, so He incorporated them into his garments so He would never be forced to take his life.

This revelation is even deeper. The pomegranates

or fruit had to be of different colors. The bells had to be of pure gold because they represents something very valuable. The fruits had to be of many colors because they represented God's many promises. Remember, Joseph's coat was made of many colors representing that through him all his family was going to be saved. Do you remember Noah's rainbow and how God set it in the sky to remember the promise He had made to Noah about never destroying the Earth again with water? The reason why the bells and pomegranates of many colors had to be together was that God was trying to reveal to us that IN YOUR PRAISE LIES THE FRUIT OF YOUR PROMISE!

Every time you praise God He is forced to remember the promises He made you throughout His Word. Promises like the thousands that are in the Bible:

Joshua 24:15 **"As for me and my house, we will**

serve the Lord."

Isaiah 53:5 "..and with His stripes we are healed."

John 10:10 "I am come that they might have life, and that they might have it more abundantly."

Luke 10:19 "Behold, I give unto you power to tread on serpents and scorpions, and over all the power of the enemy: and nothing shall by any means hurt you."

Psalm 139:14 "I am fearfully and wonderfully made."

Lamentations 3:22-23 "It is of the Lord's mercies that we are not consumed, because his compassions fail not. They are new every morning: great is thy faithfulness."

Romans 8:28 **"And we know that all things work together for good to them that love God, to them who are the called according to His purpose."**

Do you see how God established the importance of continually praising Him from the beginning, when he was dealing with Moses? Aaron was only a type of the One that was to come, our Lord Jesus Christ.

14
Who Touched Me?

D o you remember the story about the woman who had the issue of blood? She said that if she could just touch the hem of Christ's garment, she would be healed. Let's get a more complete understanding of what took place with this woman.

And a certain woman, which had an issue of blood twelve years, and had suffered many things of many physicians, and had spent all that she had, and was nothing bettered, but rather grew worse, when she had heard of Jesus, came in the press behind, and touched his garment. For she said, "If I may touch but his clothes, I shall be whole." And straightway the fountain of her blood was dried up; and

she felt in her body that she was healed of that plague. And Jesus, immediately knowing in himself that virtue had gone out of him, turned him about in the press, and said, "Who touched my clothes?"

And his disciples said unto him, "Thou seest the multitude thronging thee, and sayest thou, Who touched me?" And he looked round about to see her that had done this thing. But the woman fearing and trembling, knowing what was done in her, came and fell down before him, and told him all the truth. And he said unto her, "Daughter, thy faith hath made thee whole; go in peace, and be whole of thy plague." (Mark 5:25-34)

Mark explains fully what happened with this woman. First of all, she was an outcast because she had an issue of blood. Everyone considered whatever she touched contaminated. She was ignored by everyone because she had this issue for 12 years. The number 12 represents government, implying that she was governed, or controlled, by this disease. No one could help her, but rather she grew worse. Have you been in a situation where no one could help you and everything was just getting worse?

In verse 27 it says she heard about Jesus and came behind Him in the crowd and touched His garment. Jesus represents the church and the crowd are all those members trying to press in to get their needs fulfilled. Notice the revelation that this woman gives to us upon touching His garment. She was immediately healed. That is to say that her need was immediately met.

Think back to Aaron, who again, is a type of Jesus Christ. What was at the bottom of his garments? Bells and fruits. Aaron was a type of Jesus because he was the High Priest of Israel and Jesus is the High

Priest of the world. Aaron wore his priestly garment with bells and fruits. The bells represented praise. The fruit represented the life lived in the Spirit. The bells and the fruits hung at the hem.

Upon touching Jesus' hem, this woman did what everyone else failed to do: she deeply touched the Lord. According to the disciples, everyone was touching Him. The woman, by her touch, drew virtue from glory; which means power or life. Jesus said it in verse 30:

"And Jesus, immediately knowing in Himself that virtue had gone out of him…"

As with this woman, when we give our Lord heartfelt praise, it deeply touches Him. Our praise opens up the heavens for us so that life through the Spirit can come down. Many people touched Jesus that day, but she was the only one who deeply touched Him. Upon her doing this, God remembered His promise. Psalm 91:10 "There shall no evil befall thee, neither shall any plague come nigh thy dwelling." Remember what happened in Egypt when the plagues struck but did not affect the children of Israel? This was the promise that God had established with them, and through her touch, He was forced to exercise it and bring it into existence.

Let's touch the Lord today with our heartfelt praise to Him.

15

Who's Knocking?

After the Lord finished praying, His disciples asked Him to teach them to pray. In His teaching, Jesus said to the disciples in Luke 11:9:

And I say unto you, Ask, and it shall be given you; seek, and ye shall find; knock, and it shall be opened unto you. For every one that asketh receiveth; and he that seeketh findeth; and to him that knocketh it shall be opened.

What Jesus wanted to explain to the disciples were the three divine steps to getting a hold of the spirit. Notice how he starts by saying, **"ask and it shall be given you."** This represents going before God in prayer. Next He says, **"Seek and ye shall**

find." This represents seeking in the Word. John 5:39 says, **"Search the scriptures; for in them ye think ye have eternal life: and they are they which testify of me."** Finally, He completes the final step, which I want you to pay close attention to. **"Knock, and it will be opened."** Have you ever gone to someone's house to pay them a visit and knocked to let the person on the inside hear through the sound that you are on the outside? Now think about what Jesus said to Phillip and the disciples in John 14:3:

> **In My Father's house are many mansions: if it were not so, I would have told you. I go to prepare a place for you.**

Most mansions have a doorbell that makes a distinct sound throughout the house, alerting the owner wherever he is that someone is at the door. Regarding God's house in the book of Exodus, bells represented praise:

A golden bell and a pomegranate, a golden bell and a pomegranate, upon the hem of the robe round about. And it shall be upon Aaron to minister: and his sound shall be heard when he goeth in unto the holy place before the Lord, and when he cometh out, that he die not. (Exodus 28:34-35)

So, to tie everything together, as we praise Him, it shall be opened unto you. What shall be opened unto you is probably the question you are asking yourself right about now. The answer is this: the windows of heaven. God will pour out a blessing that you will not have enough room to contain.

There was a divine sequence here that Jesus wants you to follow. The first thing He wants you to do is ask God to give you understanding of the promises of Scripture so you can praise Him continuously. This way all the doors that concealed His promises for your life may be opened unto you.

16

Praise is Where it Started

Genesis 1:1-3 will give us a deeper understanding regarding the Garments of Praise.

In the beginning, God created the heaven and the earth. And the earth was without form and void, and darkness was upon the face of the deep. And the Spirit of God moved upon the face of the waters. And God said, "Let there be light:" and there was light.

God, in these three verses, represents a shadow of what happens when you praise God. The Scripture says, **"And the Spirit of God moved upon the face of the waters."** My question is, why did it move upon the face of the waters? Go to Psalm 148:4, 7:

Praise him, ye heavens of heavens, and ye waters that be above the heavens... Praise the Lord from the earth, ye dragons, and all deeps.

If you connect this to what it says in Genesis 2, the reason the Spirit of God was moving upon the face of the waters was because the waters drew Him down through their praise, and whenever you draw God with praise, virtue must come out of Him. This is why verse 3 says, **"And God said, 'Let there be light.'"** Jesus said, **"The words that I speak are spirit and life,"** but before God speaks on your behalf, you have to speak on His behalf. Hence Galatians 6:7-8 says,

Be not deceived; God is not mocked: for whatsoever a man soweth, that shall he also

reap. For he that soweth to his flesh shall of the flesh reap corruption; but he that soweth to the Spirit shall of the Spirit reap life everlasting.

God is letting us know that we sow with our lips. If people sow fleshly praise, which is self-glorification, they will reap from their flesh corruption. Subsequently, many young people have to listen to worldly music before they do something bad. They are sowing through their praise to the enemy, and from the enemy, are reaping corruption.

Much of today's music is designed by the enemy so that you can sing the words that are in the music and reap the same harvest. That is why young people listen to an erotic song before engaging in a sexual act, because their praise is sowing into their flesh and they will reap what they have sown. The enemy took this from God because God established in His Word that based on how you bless Him, He is going to bless you. Accordingly Jesus said in Matthew 10:33,

Whosoever shall deny me before men, him will I also deny before my Father which is in heaven.

Be certain that if you praise Him before men, He will acknowledge you before the Father and His angels. In Genesis 1, the Earth, the depths, and the waters had to praise God before God could acknowledge them by bringing them forth. He acknowledged them and brought them forth by saying, **"Let there be light."** We represent the Earth that is without form, void, and in darkness. By lifting up our voice to God, it activates Him to speak life into our situations. The Scriptures say in 1 Corinthians 12:3:

Wherefore, I give you to understand, that no man speaking by the Spirit of God calleth

Jesus accursed: and that no man can say that Jesus is the Lord, but by the Holy Ghost.

This teaches us that upon exalting God through our spirit and praise, He will exalt us out of our situation. The woman with the issue of blood represented a person who was without form, void, and in darkness, but was made whole because she touched God. She was no longer formless, but a new creature. She was no longer void, but instead filled with the Spirit. She was no longer in darkness, but now gave off light.

Keep in mind that all of this occurred as a result of her receiving a revelation that if her touching God can't do it, nothing can. Put on the garments of praise so you too can touch the Living God. Shout, for the Lord has given you the victory!

About the Author

Evangelist Matias Rojas is a spirit-filled man who is being used powerfully to reach the lost for the Kingdom of God. He has dedicated the last 16 years of his life to full time ministry. Evangelist Matias studied at Zion Bible College (now Northpoint Bible College) and graduated with a double Bachelor's. He also attended Asbury Theological Seminary in the M.Div. program. As he has studied to show himself approved, the Lord has been using him mightily from coast to coast in the nation and as well as internationally. Some of the places he has been to preach the Gospel are: Dominican Republic, Haiti, Tanzania, Burundi, Puerto Rico, Guatemala, India, Dubai, South Korea, Liberia, Columbia, Canada, Panama, and Mexico.

Evangelist Matias leads mission teams to the nations every month to hold evangelistic crusades and serve the most vulnerable demographics. Dental clinics, grocery giveaways, school and orphanage funding, and the distribution of clothing, laptops, stoves, refrigerators, washing machines, motorcycles, and cars are some of activities uses to reach the nations. In 2021, Evangelist Matias was able to successfully complete 12 crusades, preach to over 45,000 people in other nations, and saw over 25,000 salvations accompanied by healings, signs, and wonders. M.O.R.E. Ministries funds a Christian school in Dominican Republic which educates over 200 children. The ministry also currently has 9 churches under its covering in various locations.

Evangelist Matias is married to his wife, Pastor Lydia Rojas, and they have three beautiful children, Jeremiah, Sophia, and Wonderful Grace Rojas. Evangelist Matias and Pastor Lydia serve on the staff of House of Prayer Church of Waterbury, CT, under the spiritual covering of Pastor James and Verna Lilley. They reside in Terryville, Connecticut, where they have established their ministry headquarters and host monthly partnership conferences.

WWW.MIMINISTRIES.ORG

About MORE International Ministries

Mission

MORE International Ministries is committed to proclaiming the Gospel, serving the most vulnerable, and educating the next generation of servant-leaders.

Vision

Abundant Life for All

Goals

Establish a global ministry that proclaims the Gospel in the most needed places of the world.

Establish centers of education, training, and service in strategic locations in developing countries.

Mentor and develop indigenous leaders for holistic ministry in his or her respective country.

The Mission Strategies
of MORE International Ministries

Spiritual Impartation

M.O.R.E. International Ministries has as a fundamental commitment to preach a holistic Gospel to the whole world. This goal is accomplished through a variety of methods, such as…

Outreach Rallies, Crusades, Festivals, Leadership Development, Evangelism Conferences

Social Transformation

Develop sustainable projects that will assists the flourishing of families and children in developing countries.

Engagement and empowerment of youth through sports camps and outreach activities.

Sustainable Education

Develop local schools, wells,

and other building projects in developing countries.

WWW.MIMINISTRIES.ORG

Made in the USA
Middletown, DE
29 October 2023

41408823R00050